Inside Stuff
The Seattle Mariners' luxury clubhouse includes a new carpet with the team logo, leather couches, and eight flat-screen TVs. The players wear white or teal jerseys for home games and navy shirts for batting practice. Star slugger Robinson Cano gets VIP treatment — two lockers and a corner spot so he can see everyone who enters the room.

Sports Illustrated KIDS

ALL NEW ACCESS

Bird Calls
St. Louis Cardinals mascot Fredbird kicks back and relaxes in the locker room before a game.

Managing Editor, Sports Illustrated Kids Mark Bechtel

Project Editors Andrea Woo, Sachin Shenolikar,
Julia Morrill

Creative Director Beth Bugler

Designer Kirsten Sorton

Director of Photography Marguerite Schropp Lucarelli

Photo Editor Annmarie Avila

Writers Gary Gramling, Vidur Malik, Christina M. Tapper

Copy Editor Katherine Pradt

Premedia Geoffrey Michaud, Dan Larkin,
Gerry Burke, Sandra Vallejos

TIME HOME ENTERTAINMENT

Publisher Jim Childs
Vice President, Brand & Digital Strategy Steven Sandonato
Executive Director, Marketing Services Carol Pittard
Executive Director, Retail & Special Sales Tom Mifsud
Executive Publishing Director Joy Bomba
Director, Bookazine Development & Marketing Laura Adam
Vice President, Finance Vandana Patel
Publishing Director Megan Pearlman
Assistant General Counsel Simone Procas
Assistant Director, Special Sales Ilene Schreider
Senior Book Production Manager Susan Chodakiewicz
Brand Manager Jonathan White
Associate Prepress Manager Alex Voznesenskiy
Associate Project Manager Stephanie Braga

Editorial Director Stephen Koepp
Senior Editor Roe D'Angelo
Copy Chief Rina Bander
Design Manager Anne-Michelle Gallero
Editorial Operations Gina Scauzillo

Special thanks: Katherine Barnet, Brad Beatson, Jeremy Biloon, Rose Cirrincione, Assu Etsubneh, Mariana Evans, Christine Font, Susan Hettleman, Hillary Hirsch, David Kahn, Amy Mangus, Kimberly Marshall, Nina Mistry, Dave Rozzelle, Ricardo Santiago, Adriana Tierno

Copyright © 2014 Time Home Entertainment Inc.
Published by Time Home Entertainment Inc.
1271 Ave of the Americas, 6th Floor
New York, New York 10020

ISBN 10: 1-61893-049-4
ISBN 13: 978-1-61893-049-1
Library of Congress Control Number: 2014934079

Sports Illustrated Kids is a trademark of Time Inc.

We welcome your comments and suggestions about Sports Illustrated Kids Books.
Please write to us at:
Sports Illustrated Kids Books
Attention: Book Editors
P.O. Box 11016
Des Moines, IA 50336-1016

If you would like to order any of our hardcover Collector's Edition books, please call us at
1-800-327-6388 (Monday through Friday, 7 a.m.–8 p.m., or Saturday,
7 a.m.–6 p.m., Central Time).

1 TLF 14

Stacked Up

Did you know that more than 700,000 footballs are made per year at the Wilson factory? Check out every detail of the process — from the leather arriving at the factory to the balls being laced up for game day.

ATHLETES

GO BEHIND THE SCENES WITH THE BIGGEST STARS IN SPORTS

SECTION 123 ROW 01 SEAT 06

ALL ACCESS

ALL ACCESS

The Model QB

Piece by piece, Lego Master Builder Erik Varszegi designed a bust of Carolina Panthers quarterback Cam Newton in brick form. He reveals the secrets of the process

All in the Details

Getting Newton's eyes and teeth perfect was a painstaking process. "I sit down with a bunch of Lego elements and begin forming key parts of my model's face, adding and taking away bricks until I get the proper shape," says Varszegi.

Glued In

How do you keep 25,000 little bricks from coming apart? "We use special glue that we mix in house to keep the bricks together," Varszegi says. "The main purpose of it is to keep the model together during shipping and handling."

CAM NEWTON
Quarterback, Carolina Panthers

In his first three NFL seasons, Newton had 11,299 passing yards and 92 total touchdowns. He was named the 2011 AP Offensive Rookie of the Year.

Putting in the Time

The Newton model was designed and built in July 2012. The design took 40 hours. Once it was finalized, Varszegi turned over much of the construction to an assistant in the Lego Model Shop (below). After 55 hours of building, Lego Cam was finally finished.

JOE JOHNSON
Guard, Brooklyn Nets

A seven-time NBA All-Star, Johnson has a career average of 17.5 points a game over 13 seasons for Brooklyn, Atlanta, Phoenix, and Boston.

A Secret Sneaker Haven!

A hidden door leads to Brooklyn Nets guard Joe Johnson's shoe closet, which is filled with hundreds of his favorite kicks

⟫ Not Just For Kicks

Johnson has 200–250 pairs of sneakers in his basement closet, but the space isn't just a shoe cave. His framed Arkansas Razorbacks jersey is a nod to his college days, and the mini basketball hoop offers a chance for some game action. "My son and I play around with the hoop that's in there, so [the room] is a place for fun too," he says.

⟪ Keeping Track

Johnson relies on his memory to keep track of all of his sneakers, but he admits he doesn't remember every shoe he owns. "I've definitely looked at a pair in the closet and said 'I forgot about these!'" he says with a laugh.

⌄ Shh . . . It's a Secret

The closet is hidden behind a door that resembles a wall and is only accessible through a fingerprint scanner. "It's high-tech and James Bond-ish," he says. "Once you enter, you're surprised at the [amount of] space."

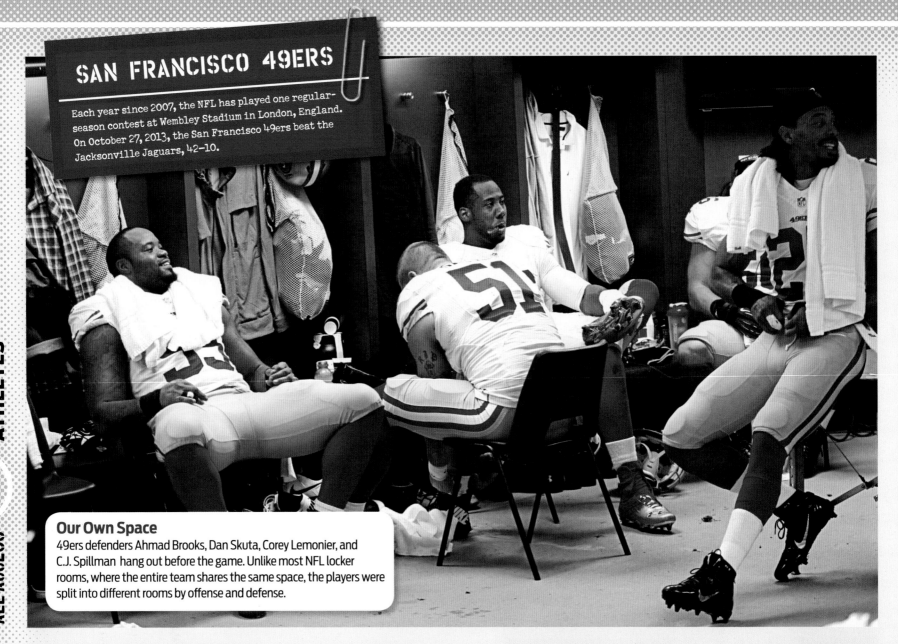

Each year since 2007, the NFL has played one regular-season contest at Wembley Stadium in London, England. On October 27, 2013, the San Francisco 49ers beat the Jacksonville Jaguars, 42–10.

Our Own Space
49ers defenders Ahmad Brooks, Dan Skuta, Corey Lemonier, and C.J. Spillman hang out before the game. Unlike most NFL locker rooms, where the entire team shares the same space, the players were split into different rooms by offense and defense.

Pregame Crunch

An inside look at how the Niners prepared in the locker room before their big win in London

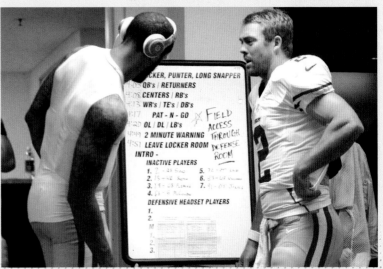

»» On-Time Arrival
With more than 50 players to manage, NFL teams follow rigid, down-to-the-minute schedules to make sure every aspect of game day goes smoothly. In this photo, quarterbacks Colin Kaepernick and Colt McCoy look at a whiteboard that tells players when they should report to the field.

Pep Talk
49ers coach Jim Harbaugh gives his team a final message before they take the field. A few hours later, they would get Harbaugh one of his 36 career regular-season wins.

Clothes Calls
Players wear several layers of pads, so it can take a while to prepare and get dressed for a game. Here, Kaepernick gets his hip pads ready.

Spin Cycle
Kaepernick listens to music and rides a stationary bike to relax and warm up in the locker room. His pregame routine worked: Kaepernick rushed for two touchdowns and passed for another in the game.

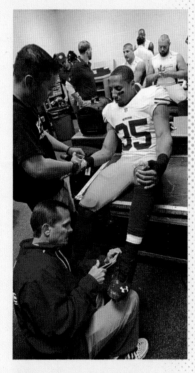

Pump It Up
Team equipment managers make sure every part of a player's uniform fits perfectly, from jerseys to shoulders pads to shoes. In this photo, equipment staffer Robert Lloyd pumps air into safety Eric Reid's helmet to ensure a snug fit.

Tale of the Tape
Even after putting on their uniforms, players like Reid aren't done dressing. Here, trainers Manny Rivera (standing) and Jeff Ferguson apply athletic tape on the safety's hands and feet to provide cushioning and support.

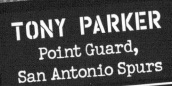

TONY PARKER
Point Guard,
San Antonio Spurs

Parker has been a starter for San Antonio since 2001. He is the all-time franchise leader in assists and ranks fourth in points scored.

Home Hardware

The future Hall of Famer gave a tour of the trophy room in his home

Winning Number
Parker made his NBA debut in the number 9 jersey at age 19 years and 166 days, becoming the youngest player to appear in a game with the Spurs. He now ranks third in team history in games played.

Ringing It In
Parker has three NBA championship rings from Spurs titles in the 2002–03, 2004–05, and 2006–07 seasons. He came within seconds of winning a fourth ring in 2012–13, but the Miami Heat came from behind to win Game 6 of the NBA Finals and then clinched the title in Game 7.

Star Among Stars
Parker has also showcased his talent at All-Star Saturday Night. He won trophies for winning the Skills Challenge ball-handling and shooting competition in 2012 and the Shooting Stars contest (teaming up with WNBA star Kendra Wecker and NBA legend Steve Kerr) in 2006.

Leading Man
After years of being treated as an intern for center Tim Duncan, Parker finally became the Spurs' go-to guy. In 2007, he was awarded this trophy after being named the Most Valuable Player of the NBA Finals. He averaged 24.5 points and 3.25 assists in the Spurs' four-game sweep of the Cleveland Cavaliers.

First of Many
This is Parker's jersey from the 2006 NBA All-Star game. He scored just eight points and committed five turnovers in the game, but it still has special meaning for him: It was his first All-Star game. He has played in five more since then.

Pride of His Country
Before Parker, there were few players from France in the NBA. He has helped his home country reach new heights in international basketball, leading France to a gold medal and being named MVP at the 2013 FIBA Europe EuroBasket championship. He also helped his squad to a silver medal in 2011 and a bronze in 2005.

Queen of the Hill

Mikaela Shiffrin has had quite a start to her career. In 2013, she won four World Cup slalom races and gold at the world championships. The 19-year-old followed up with a gold-medal peformance at the 2014 Winter Olympics.

A phenom on the slopes since she was a kid, Shiffrin has no shortage of natural talent. She has combined that ability with smart training, rigorous studying, and a proper diet to take her skiing to a world-class level. We asked Shiffrin to explain how she prepares her body and mind for races.

MIKAELA SHIFFRIN
Alpine Skier

In 2014, Shiffrin became the youngest woman (age 18) to win an Olympic gold medal in slalom skiing. She was also the first U.S. woman in over 40 years to win the event.

Mind Control

"If I am not fully awake and ready to charge down the hill when I get in the starting gate, then it becomes scary, especially when I'm skiing at 50 to 60 miles per hour. I do deep breathing exercises before the start of a race: I take a six-second breath in, hold it for three seconds, and then exhale for six seconds. I do that for as long as it takes to feel like I'm in control of my mind."

Fueling Up

"I usually eat two eggs, a piece of toast, and whole wheat cereal for breakfast. For lunch, I have a meat sandwich or pasta with chicken. I stick with fruits for my snacks. For dinner, I usually have a salad with grilled chicken and a small portion of pasta. My pre-race meal is a little heavier on carbs: a small salad and a bigger portion of pasta with meat sauce. I also eat pasta and meat sauce after a race for carbs and protein to rebuild my muscles."

Strength Building

"The abdominal muscles, back, and legs are probably the most important for skiing. You have to be really stable in your core to pull off a turn with a lot of force, and you have to be strong in your legs to do those kind of turns over and over again. When I'm in the gym, my workouts are based around squats and other leg-strengthening exercises."

Down Time

Pro athletes spend countless hours working on their games. After all, that's their job. But when they're away from their sport, they fill the time in different ways. Some play *other* sports as a way to relax. Some use art and music as an escape. Here's a look at the hobbies these stars enjoy when they're not scoring touchdowns or swishing three-pointers.

NAME: VERNON DAVIS
NFL Tight End

HOBBY: Painting

There's no doubt that Davis has great hands — he caught 13 touchdown passes in 2013. He is also a skilled painter who owns an art gallery in San Jose, California. Davis majored in studio art at the University of Maryland and loves to decorate his home with his paintings (below).

NAME: STEPHEN CURRY
NBA Guard

HOBBY: Golf

Curry's passion for golf has one big benefit — it's an excuse to bond with his father, Dell. "My favorite thing about golf has always been getting to spend time with my dad," he says. Curry has been hitting the links since he was a kid and played on his high school's golf team. He also enjoys keeping up with the latest news on the PGA Tour. "The TV at home is pretty much always on the Golf Channel," he says.

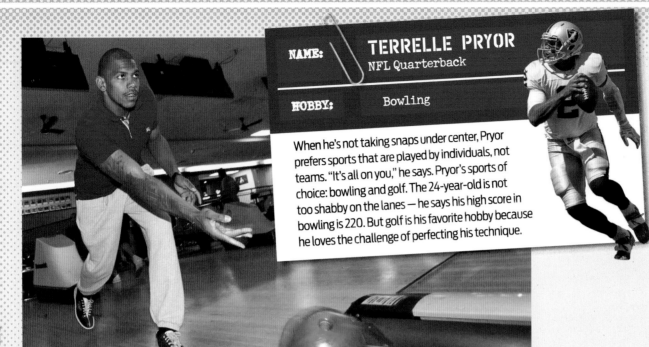

NAME: TERRELLE PRYOR
NFL Quarterback

HOBBY: Bowling

When he's not taking snaps under center, Pryor prefers sports that are played by individuals, not teams. "It's all on you," he says. Pryor's sports of choice: bowling and golf. The 24-year-old is not too shabby on the lanes — he says his high score in bowling is 220. But golf is his favorite hobby because he loves the challenge of perfecting his technique.

NAME: CHRIS JOHNSON
NFL Running Back

HOBBY: Cars

Johnson has quite the motor on the gridiron, so it's fitting that he loves to collect cars. The 28-year-old owns old-school models and newer luxury cars, many with custom paint colors and parts. His prized set of wheels is a yellow and green Chevrolet Caprice with a raised body and yellow rims. Johnson also has a toy car collection for his two sons, Chris Junior and Kaden. They ride around in miniature cars modeled after luxury convertibles.

NAME: **RAJON RONDO**
NBA Guard

HOBBY: Roller Skating

The soft-spoken Rondo isn't shy about showing off his fancy moves in the roller rink — he can do spins, skate backward, and even dribble a basketball while on wheels. The star point guard took up roller skating in 2007, during the summer after his rookie season. And just as he did on the basketball court, he got really good, really fast.

NAME: **VICTOR OLADIPO**
NBA Guard

HOBBY: Singing

Oladipo has been belting out tunes since he was a kid. "I was raised in the church, so that's how I learned to sing," he says. While in college at Indiana, his talent was uncovered when videos of him singing at school functions went viral. Oladipo loves to cover songs by R&B stars John Legend and Usher and the legendary Bill Withers.

PATRICK PETERSON
Cornerback, Arizona Cardinals

A three-time Pro Bowler, Peterson makes an impact on defense and special teams. He has 12 interceptions, nine fumble recoveries, and four punt-return TDs in his career, as of 2013.

Custom Kicks

In just three seasons, Arizona Cardinals cornerback Patrick Peterson has established himself as one of the most explosive defensive playmakers in the NFL. Peterson is a blur on the field, but the next time you watch a Cards game, see if you can catch a glimpse of his footwear. You might be surprised!

During the past two seasons, Peterson worked with artist Matt Myers to create cool custom designs for his cleats. The Mesa, Arizona–based Myers then painted them on the sneakers. "He can pretty much do anything," Peterson says of his partner's skills.

Fishy Feet

This pair is one of Peterson's favorites. The toe areas have a shark's head design, which was a common sight on the noses of fighter planes in the mid-1900s. Peterson was so impressed by the artwork that he didn't want to risk ruining it during games. "Those were *sick*," he says. "I was like, 'I'm not wearing these.'"

Peanuts Gallery

Peterson and Myers get plenty of inspiration from the holiday season. This cleat features characters from the *Peanuts* cartoon, which is famous for its Thanksgiving and Christmas TV specials. Peterson designed a football scene for Charlie Brown and his pals — and included himself in the action.

Dr.'s Orders

The Nike Huarache cleat is the canvas for all of Peterson's art projects. This pair, another holiday-themed one, features a classic Christmas villain: The Grinch. The grumpy Dr. Seuss character is dressed as a referee and is tugging on Peterson's jersey.

Fan Favorite

This cleat was inspired by the movie *The Nightmare Before Christmas*. Last December, Peterson posted a picture of two pairs of cleats on Instagram and asked his followers to vote for which one they wanted him to wear on the field. This ghoulish cleat came out on top.

Baseball Paradise

In 2011, MLB opened a three-story play space called the Fan Cave. New York Yankees pitcher CC Sabathia gives you the tour!

PLACES

SOME OF THE COOLEST STUFF IN SPORTS IS BEHIND CLOSED DOORS

SECTION 206   ROW 03   SEAT 10

ALL ACCESS

Game Time
No matter which team you cheer for, you will never miss a game in the Fan Cave. Here, Sabathia and his son, CC III — aka Lil' C — kick back near a wall of 15 46-inch HD televisions that show every MLB game that is being played.

It's a Party!
The lower level of the cave is a huge event space where fans can hang out and talk baseball. When guests aren't debating who's the best team in the majors, they can create music playlists in the DJ booth or grab the mic of the karaoke machine.

Family Photo
No visit to the Fan Cave is complete without a trip to the photo booth. Sabathia takes a break from all the fun to smile for the camera with Lil' C and his sister, Sabathia's daughter Jaden.

Total Control
The Mission Control station features 30 screens that provide windows into every MLB ballpark on game day. Fan Cave visitors can find out the weather for each game and scroll through Instagram posts.

Corner Pocket
A fierce competitor, Sabathia always wears his game face — even when he's playing Lil' C in a friendly game of pool. "Whether it's pool or video games, I don't let this kid beat me at anything," Sabathia says. This custom billiards table includes balls for all 30 major league teams.

Home Run Slide

As a starting pitcher in the American League, Sabathia rarely reaches for a bat because of the designated hitter rule. But he couldn't resist playing around with this oversized toy near the 10-foot tall home run slide. "Holding this bat feels weird," Sabathia says. "I'm not used to this!"

New Heights

A highlight in 2013 was Nonopus, a big orange octopus. It's called a Nonopus to honor the pitching milestone of a no-hitter ("no-no"-pus, get it?). This Nonopus is named Homer after Cincinnati Reds flamethrower Homer Bailey, the first pitcher to throw a no-hitter in 2013.

Wall of Fame

Take a close look at this wall of more than 600 Rawlings baseballs and you'll notice that each is signed by an athlete or celebrity who has visited the Fan Cave. "It's pretty cool to spot different signatures, like [Los Angeles Dodgers outfielder] Yasiel Puig and [rapper] B.O.B.," says Lil' C.

King Pong

An ace on the mound, Sabathia shows Lil' C how to serve up an ace while playing table tennis. "The Fan Cave has so much to offer," Lil' C says. "It's a great place and you'll have fun during each and every visit. I love it here."

Super Bowl Confidential

How did the Seahawks and the Broncos prepare for the game of their lives? Hoops, haircuts, and having fun, for starters

The Place to Be
The game, at MetLife Stadium in East Rutherford, New Jersey, was the first Super Bowl in an open-air venue in a cold-weather city. Weeks before kickoff, the forecast showed a snowstorm, but the NFL lucked out — the conditions were perfect for the players and the more than 80,000 fans who attended.

》 For Pete's Sake
Seahawks coach Pete Carroll is one of the most energetic and physically fit coaches in the game. Here, he passes the time before the first team meeting by working on his jump shot.

Hot Shot
Ever since his stellar rookie season in 2012, Seahawks quarterback Russell Wilson has been in the spotlight. Even his teammates wanted to take photos of the talented passer, who posed in front of cameras during media day.

Game Face

Fullback Michael Robinson (left) and masked-man running back Marshawn Lynch took a break from bulldozing defenders in the locker room. In the Super Bowl, Lynch was still a scary sight, rushing for 39 yards and a touchdown on 15 carries.

Time for a Trim

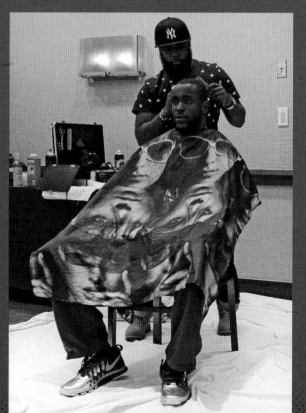

The week leading up to the Super Bowl isn't just about preparing for what happens on the field. Players make sure to take care of themselves off the field, too. Seahawks strong safety Kam Chancellor got a haircut a few days before the big game. Chancellor went on to give a dominant performance, recording five tackles and an interception.

Strike a Pose

Cornerback Richard Sherman (middle) stayed loose while chilling with his teammates. Sherman, who proclaimed himself the best corner in the NFL, hurt his knee during the Super Bowl, but throughout the season, he was a key part of Seattle's physical secondary.

›› Livin' It
Quarterback Peyton Manning (left) and cornerback Champ Bailey took some time to kick back and relax. For the two future Hall of Famers, the Super Bowl was a chance to build on their already impressive legacies.

›› How Do I Look?
The players gathered in front of a mirror to primp before their team portrait.

⌃ Name of the Game
Safety David Bruton made sure everyone saw his name atop his locker. Bruton, who starred for Notre Dame in college, is a captain of the Broncos and a special teams standout.

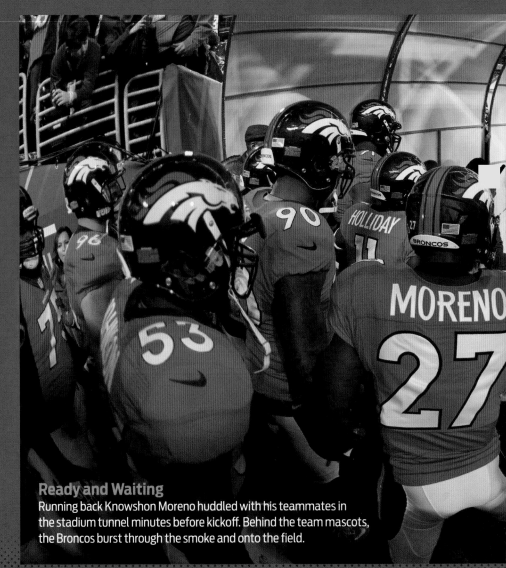

Ready and Waiting
Running back Knowshon Moreno huddled with his teammates in the stadium tunnel minutes before kickoff. Behind the team mascots, the Broncos burst through the smoke and onto the field.

Happy Days

Peyton Manning and Denver coach John Fox shared a light moment. Though they weren't as cheerful after the Broncos' loss, both Fox and Manning are among the league's best, and Denver has a strong chance to go back to the Super Bowl.

Say Cheese

Though the Broncos were preparing for a team photo, linebacker Nate Irving wanted to be the center of attention. But when he laid down, not everyone was laughing — Peyton Manning (right end of the second row) doesn't look like he approves of Irving's antics!

BIGFOOT 4X4 GARAGE
Hazelwood, Missouri

Take a peek at the place where monster trucks are built, fixed up, and fine-tuned.

Big Wheels

Weighing 11,000 pounds with tires more than five feet high, BIGFOOT monster trucks can crush anything in their path. The BIGFOOT, which was built more than three decades ago, is considered the original monster truck. Bob Chandler, the founder of the BIGFOOT 4x4 facility, is credited with inventing the supersized trucks. Today, BIGFOOT maintains 20 trucks that compete in about 1,000 races per year.

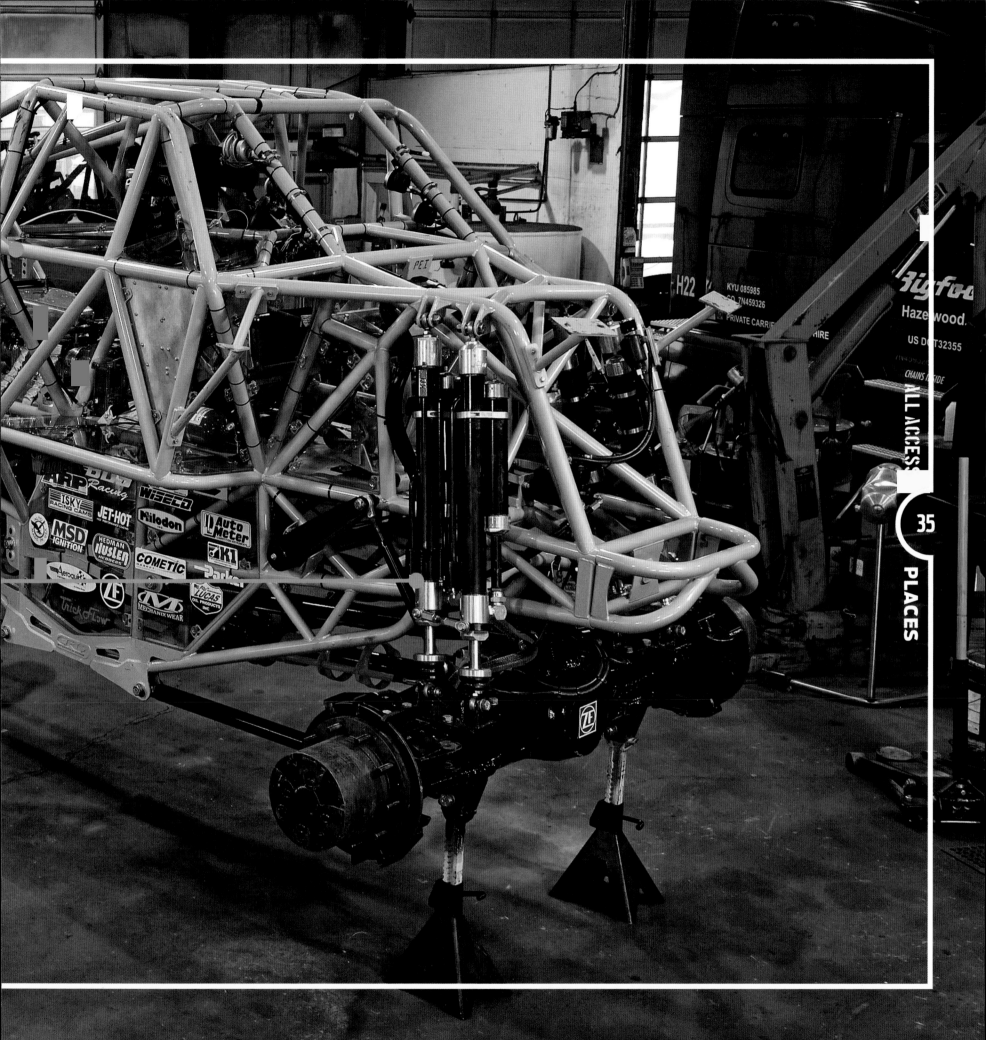

Causing a Spark

BIGFOOT mechanic Larry Swim works on a truck axle. Monster trucks have super-sized axles, which sit under the frame and connect the wheels to the frame.

Bright Ideas

Painter Nick Dvorchak applies a base coat to a truck body. Though they're known for the way they move, BIGFOOT trucks are also works of art. Truck bodies go through several rounds of painting, waxing, and buffing to make them shine.

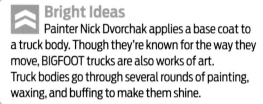

View from Above

Each truck has a custom-designed seat with a neck brace for driver safety. A transparent floorboard lets drivers see what they drive over.

Frame of the Game

Darron Schnell (left) and JR Adams (right) install a truck body on a BIGFOOT frame. These are made of fiberglass, which is a light material that is easier to work with than metal. The frames get worn down during races, and they last only a few months.

Routine Check-up

Much of the work at the BIGFOOT shop goes into maintaining the monster trucks, which can take a beating during shows. Mechanic John Peterson checks an engine.

Carrying the Load

Larry Swim installs a four-link bar, a major part of the BIGFOOT's suspension system. Suspension is important because BIGFOOT trucks weigh more than five tons!

Manning the Controls

Darron Schnell replaces a BIGFOOT's heim joints, which are part of the truck's steering system.

Nearing the Finish Line

Ron Bachmann (far left) and JR Adams (right) work on a truck's axles. With the body in place, this monster truck is almost ready to go.

Tall Tire

Bryan Bertoletti, John Peterson, and Larry Swim (from left to right) mount a tire on a BIGFOOT truck. A truck can't reach "monster" status without these giant wheels. Most BIGFOOT tires are 66 inches, or more than five feet high!

Boardroom

Travis Rice travels the world pulling off incredible snowboarding tricks. Back at his home in Jackson, Wyoming, he recently gave an inside look at the tools of his trade

TRAVIS RICE'S CABIN
Jackson, Wyoming

Make yourself at home in the digs of one of the greatest snowboarders of all time. Rice is a two-time Winter X Games gold medalist, and he co-produced the film *The Art of Flight*.

38

Wax On, Wax Off

Rice maintains all his boards himself and uses this area to wax his boards to keep them strong and running fast. The workbench is also where he stores some of the safety equipment that he uses to protect himself when he is riding in the backcountry, such as a first-aid kit and a device that sends out a signal in the event of an avalanche.

Get Your Motor Runnin'

When Rice won the gold medal in slopestyle at the 2002 Winter X Games at age 19, he spent part of his prize money on his first snowmobile. Now he keeps up to seven sleds around his house, including this Ski-Doo model, which he uses to access backcountry snowboarding terrain outside the boundaries of traditional ski resorts.

Tee Time

Rice enjoys playing golf in his free time. "Enough to stay averagely bad," he jokes. His bag includes Cleveland irons and a Titleist driver. The photograph hanging above his clubs was taken by Scott Serfais on one of the first trips for the video, *The Art of Flight*. It shows Rice riding in the Tordrillo mountain range. "I love this photo because it showcases how [great] Alaska can be," he says.

Surf's Up

"I first started getting into surfing when I was about 18 or 19, and I've been hooked ever since," says Rice, who has four surfboards hanging from the ceiling of his garage. Surfing has taken Rice to some exotic locations. He has gone to Tahiti with pro surfer Dane Reynolds and traveled to Norway to ride waves near the Arctic Circle, where he had to walk through snowbanks to reach the water.

Boarded Up

Included among the more than 60 snowboards that Rice has in his home are ones that he used to win contests on and the first board he ever designed with his sponsor Lib Tech. His boards range in size from 153 centimeters for riding rails to 164.5 centimeters for backcountry riding in Alaska. Rice estimates that he goes through about 10 boards each season. "Oftentimes I'm running into trees and rocks, so [my board is] my shield," he says. "Better the board break than me."

Long Trail

Rice bought this trailer when he started filming *Art of Flight*, which required carting hundreds of pounds of camera equipment. The trailer also made sense from an environmental standpoint. "I don't like going to the spot and five people drive their trucks with one snowmobile in each," Rice says. "This way we can cut down on the amount of vehicles we're using." The ASYMBOL sign on the side of the trailer is for a gallery that Rice opened in Jackson to showcase the work of artists and photographers.

Presto Change-O

On January 1, 2008, the NHL went outside to play. The game, at Ralph Wilson Stadium in Orchard Park, New York, drew a record crowd of 71,217 fans, and since then outdoor NHL games have become a showcase. Taking the game outside may be fun for fans, but transforming a football or baseball field into a sheet of ice also offers plenty of logistical challenges. We took a behind-the-scenes look at the 2011 Winter Classic between the Pittsburgh Penguins and the Washington Capitals.

HEINZ FIELD
Pittsburgh, Pennsylvania

The players were ready to hit the ice at 1 p.m. on game day, but unfortunatately the construction workers couldn't control the weather. Rain and unusually warm temperatures delayed the game seven hours. Still, more than 65,000 fans packed the stands to watch a 3-1 Capitals win.

4

Over nine days, the workers sprayed **20,000 gallons of misty tap water** on the surface to create a sheet that's two inches thick. That's nearly a full inch thicker than indoor arenas, to account for the possiblity of more melting.

5

The finishing touches were added: logos, lines, boards and benches. Finally, the outdoor rink looked just like the one fans normally see at Penguins games.

6

The construction team's work wasn't done yet, though. They had to get going immediately to remove the ice so the stadium could be ready to host a Steelers playoff game two weeks later.

COMERICA PARK
Detroit Tigers
Detroit, Michigan

For Tigers fans, nothing beats the Fly Ball Ferris wheel behind third base. The 50-foot wheel features cars shaped like baseballs that can seat up to five passengers.

Play Ball

Who's got the best MLB stadium? These parks make watching the national pasttime even more exciting

FERRIS WHEEL

PETCO PARK
San Diego Padres
San Diego, California

Just outside the right centerfield wall is The Beach, a giant 70-foot-long sandbox. Ticket holders get to build a castle and shout at an outfielder 50 feet away.

ROGERS CENTRE
Toronto Blue Jays
Toronto, Ontario, Canada

The best seat in baseball? Room 362 at the Renaissance Hotel in Toronto. Special guests get an exclusive look at the bullpens behind the outfield fence and both dugouts.

MARLINS PARK
Miami Marlins
Miami, Florida

A Bobblehead Museum holds 609 dolls in a two-sided, glass case. The shelves even have a vibrating mechanism so the heads on the figurines are constantly in motion!

TROPICANA FIELD
Tampa Bay Rays
St. Petersburg, Florida

Touch and feed over 30 cownose rays in a 35-foot, 10,000-gallon tank beyond the right centerfield fence. When a Rays player hits a ball into the tank, $5,000 goes to charity.

GEAR

FASCINATING FACTS AND ESSENTIAL TRIVIA ABOUT OBJECTS IN SPORTS

All Suited Up

Goaltender Martin Brodeur has spent two decades protecting the net for the New Jersey Devils. He gave SI KIDS an exclusive look at the equipment that protects him

Stick

Brodeur is known as one of the best stick-handling goalies of all time. When he's protecting the net, he grips his stick at the paddle with three fingers above, and his index finger across, the top of the paddle. "And I play with a brand new stick every game," he says.

Mask

Brodeur's mask features the New Jersey Devils' logo, but there are plenty of other personal touches. Painted on the back of his helmet are his three Stanley Cups, two gold medals, the initials of his five kids, and a photography film strip. The strip is a tribute to his late father, a former NHL photographer. If you look closely, you'll also find MB30 logos all over the mask. "Thirty of them!" says Brodeur.

Leggings

Underneath his leg pads, Brodeur wears a pair of thermal stockings. He wore his last pair of leggings for more than 15 years before switching to a new pair. They were handmade by a family member of his former teammate Craig Billington, now the assistant general manager for the Colorado Avalanche.

Ancient History

The Baseball Hall of Fame in Cooperstown, New York, is home to some of the coolest artifacts around

Big Apple Bat
Yankees shortstop Derek Jeter will one day be enshrined in Cooperstown. But for now, his bat from the 2009 World Series represents him there. Jeter had a .407 average and 11 hits during New York's six-game Series victory.

Capturing the Flag
The Yankees lost the 1922 World Series to the New York Giants, but they did win the American League title, a feat this pennant celebrates. Babe Ruth is shown second from the left.

Perfect Glove
On October 8, 1956, New York Yankees pitcher Don Larsen threw the only perfect game in World Series history, shutting out the Brooklyn Dodgers 2–0. This glove was used by legendary Yankee catcher Yogi Berra in that contest. A game ball rests inside it.

Where It Started
This ball was used in the first World Series, in 1903, between the Pittsburgh Pirates and the Boston Americans, who became the Red Sox. The Fall Classic had a best-of-eight-games format back then. Boston clinched the championship with five wins.

Watch It
This gold watch and fob belonged to shortstop Freddy Parent, who was part of the Boston team that won the first World Series, in 1903. The fob has an inscription recognizing Boston as champs.

Happy Feet
Wearing these spikes, reliever Koji Uehara tossed the final three outs of Game 6 of the 2013 World Series to help the Boston Red Sox claim their third championship in 10 seasons. It didn't take long for Uehara to retire the side, as he forced two flyouts and then struck out Matt Carpenter for the win.

Hat's Off to Mo
Legendary Yankees closer Mariano Rivera wore this hat during the 2009 World Series. He was part of the Yankees dynasty that won five World Series titles.

Giant Ring
These days, championship rings are filled with diamonds, but they were more modest in the early 20th century. This ring commemorated the Giants' World Series win in 1922 over the rival Yankees. It belonged to Kenesaw Mountain Landis, Major League Baseball's first commissioner.

Sole Power

From the earliest simple fashions to the colorful and high-tech new designs, soccer and basketball shoes have undergone constant change. Check out the latest sneaker looks and stats

20
Biggest shoe size in the NBA
Centers Robin Lopez and JaVale McGee each wear size 20, the largest in the NBA according to the SLAM footwear database. Robin's twin brother, Brook, isn't far off — he wears size 18 Adidas Crazyquicks (below).

adipure
crazyquick

14.81
Average shoe size for an NBA player
Super-tall NBA players also have enormous feet! The stat comes from SLAM magazine, which compiled every foot size in the NBA.

10.5
Smallest shoe size in NBA
At 5'9", Nate Robinson is one of the NBA's littlest guys, and his feet match. He wears a relatively tiny 10.5.

65% of NBA players – including superstars LeBron James, Kobe Bryant, and Kevin Durant – **wear Nike shoes.** Nike's Hyperdunk and Hyperfuse models are the two most popular sneakers in the league.

15% of NBA players, including All-Stars Derrick Rose and Dwight Howard, **wear Adidas shoes.** International brands are also making inroads: Dwyane Wade wears Li-Ning and Kevin Garnett wears Anta.

Brazilian legend Pelé controls the ball during a 1966 World Cup match.

Fashion Forward

In the mid-20th century, cleats looked much different than they do today. They were made from leather, which felt comfortable but did not hold up in the elements. "If you wore a shoe from the '50s, they would get really bogged down in wet weather and stretch quite a bit," said Tor Southard, the senior merchandise manager for Adidas soccer.

Like basketball shoes, sales of soccer cleats exploded with marketing the sport's best athletes. Pelé, perhaps the best soccer player of all time, participated in the trend by sporting the Puma King during the 1970 World Cup.

In the '90s, a new cleat changed the way soccer shoes were made. The Adidas Predator, which was released in 1994, featured a mix of rubber and leather that gave players much more control with the ball. The Predator, David Beckham's shoe of choice, has since gone on to be one of the most popular cleats.

Puma King

Today, technology has improved, and the game has become faster. The newest models help players control the ball at high speeds. For example, the Adidas Adizero F50 — worn by Barcelona star Lionel Messi — is lightweight and created with materials that feel like leather but are more durable. And the Nitrocharge (left) has tiny elastic springs in the sole that increase a player's momentum.

Adidas Predator

Adidas Adizero F50

Etched In Silver

Every NHL champion gets their name engraved on the Stanley Cup. Here are some of the best (and wackiest) stories behind the names, along with must-know facts about the most famous trophy in sports.

Different Jersey, Same Cup

Ten players have their names on the Cup with three or more teams. The most recent was right wing Mark Recchi (right), who won it with the Pittsburgh Penguins (1990–91), Carolina Hurricanes (2005–06), and Boston Bruins ('10–11).

Spelling Errors

Winning the championship doesn't mean that teams will be immortalized correctly on the Cup. Three team names are misspelled on the trophy: the 1962–63 Toronto Maple Leafs (LEAES), the '71–72 Boston Bruins (BQSTON), and the '80–81 New York Islanders (ILANDERS).

Not Just a Boys' Club

Sixteen women have their names engraved on the Stanley Cup. Detroit Red Wings president Marguerite Norris was the first, in 1953–54.

X Marks the Spot

After winning the Stanley Cup in 1983–84, Edmonton Oilers owner Peter Pocklington included his father, Basil, on the list of names to be added to the trophy. Since Basil was unaffiliated with the team, the NHL later had his name covered with X's.

Repeat Performance

Henri Richard of the Montreal Canadiens (above, left) has his name carved in the Cup 11 times, more than any other player. His teammate Jean Beliveau appears the most overall, 17. He's on it 10 times as a player and seven as a member of the Canadiens' front office.

Not Messing Around

Mark Messier (right) is the only player to captain two different Cup-winning teams: the 1989–90 Edmonton Oilers and the '93–94 New York Rangers.

Jacques With a "Q"

Goalie Jacques Plante won the Stanley Cup with the Montreal Canadiens for five straight years from 1956 through '60. Somehow, the engraver never learned his name. It is spelled differently each time. Adam Deadmarsh, who won the Cup with the Colorado Avalanche in '95–96, was the first player to have his misspelling (DEADMARCH) corrected.

Youth Is Served

Sidney Crosby of the Pittsburgh Penguins (above, right) didn't waste time making his mark on history. In 2008–09, his fourth NHL season, Crosby became the youngest player (age 21) to captain a team to a title.

Where's Stanley?

The person for whom the Cup is named, Lord Stanley of Preston, was the Governor General of Canada and purchased the original trophy in 1892. But he never saw the Cup awarded because he moved to England before the season ended.

Carving Club

Stanley Cup winners are an elite group, but the list of people who have etched the names on the Cup is even smaller. Since 1907, the first year names were put on the Cup, only four people have been the official engraver. The job is held currently by Louise St. Jacques (left).

Long List

Can you guess how many names fit on the 35¼-inch-tall Stanley Cup? The answer: 2,372. The first team to engrave its roster on the trophy was the 1906–07 Montreal Wanderers. Older bands on the Cup's barrel are removed to make room for bands with the most recent winners. The '97–98 Red Wings team (above) had the most names etched on the Cup (55).

The Making Of a Football

Ada, Ohio, doesn't stick out on a map. The town with a population of about 6,000 is a two-and-a-half-hour drive from Cleveland and is tucked away in the quiet countryside of the Midwest. But there's some significant work happening in Ada — it's the location of the Wilson factory where NFL footballs are made. Since 1955, every NFL ball has been made in this facility. Today, it employs 120 workers and produces more than 700,000 footballs per year. The Wilson staff gave SI KIDS an exclusive look at how the footballs you see on any given Sunday are made.

» 1 Hide and Seek

Each month, the factory receives the hides of 12,000 cows. Before arriving at the plant, the leather on each hide is tanned and pebbled (which creates the bumpy surface), so it's ready to be worked on as soon as it reaches the Wilson factory.

≫ 2 Making the Cut

The first step at the Wilson factory is called cutting. A handheld device is used to slice away panels. Four panels make up one football, and each hide produces 10 balls.

≋9 Lace 'Em Up Laces are attached to the ball by hand. The person manning this station tapes his fingers. "By pulling on those laces all day they can get blisters," says Riegle. "They put tape on their fingers so they don't get hurt."

≋8 A Good Turnover The balls are flipped right-side out in a process called turning. "That's the first time it looks like a football," says Riegle. After the balls are turned, it's time to put in the bladder, which holds the air. Each football has an opening by the laceholes. The bladder is inserted through that hole and then locked into place. In just a few short steps, the process of making a football will be complete.

≫10 Full of Hot Air This machine pumps 100 pounds of air pressure into the mold of the ball, straightening out its seams and making its shape uniform. The air is then sucked out to 13 pounds of pressure so the ball settles at its game weight of 14 ounces.

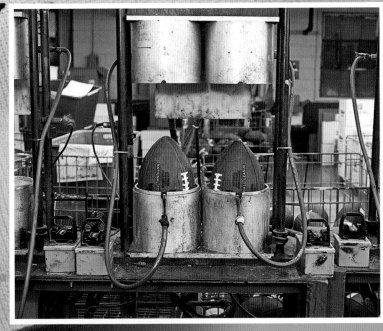

≋11 Ready for Action! After being weighed and measured, the balls are ready to be shipped to NFL teams. "It makes you very proud to know that a product you're making is used by the best professionals in the world in that sport," says Riegle.

Image Credits

COVER Heinz Kluetmeier/Sports Illustrated (door)

INSIDE COVER Ben VanHouten for Sports Illustrated

TITLE PAGE Robert Beck/Sports Illustrated

TABLE OF CONTENTS David E. Klutho/Sports Illustrated

CAM NEWTON (PAGES 4-7) Al Tielemans/Sports Illustrated (action); Michael J. LeBrecht II for Sports Illustrated (Lego bust front, Newton portrait); Damian Strohmeyer/Sports Illustrated (Lego bust back, Lego headquarters)

JOE JOHNSON (PAGES 8-9) Zach Wolfe for Sports Illustrated

SAN FRANCISCO 49ERS (PAGES 10-11) Michael Zagaris/San Francisco 49ers/Getty Images

TONY PARKER (PAGES 12-13) John W. McDonough/Sports Illustrated (Spurs); Bob Rosato/Sports Illustrated (with trophy); Christof Koepsel/Bongarts/Getty Images (France); Greg Nelson for Sports Illustrated (house); Masters of Design (rings)

MIKALA SHIFFRIN (PAGES 14-17) Simon Bruty/Sports Illustrated (Shiffrin); John Walker (Shiffrin illustration)

ATHLETE HOBBIES (PAGES 18-21) Robert Beck/Sports Illustrated (Davis); Courtesy Vernon Davis (dog painting); Jeff Gross/Getty Images (Davis action); Deanne Fitzmaurice (Curry); John W. McDonough/Sports Illustrated (Curry action); Jod Jacobsohn for Sports Illustrated (Pryor); David E. Klutho/Sports Illustrated (Pryor action); Jeffery A. Salter for Sports Illustrated (Johnson); Bob Rosato/Sports Illustrated (Johnson action); Bill Frakes/Sports Illustrated (Oladipo); Fernando Medina/NBAE/Getty Images (Oladipo action); Michael J. LeBrecht II for Sports Illustrated (Rondo); Nathanial S. Butler/NBAE/Getty Images (Rondo action)

PATRICK PETERSON (PAGES 22-23) Kohjiro Kinno for Sports Illustrated

MLB FAN CAVE (PAGES 24–27) Heinz Kluetmeier for Sports Illustrated (Sabathia); Elsa/Getty Images (MLB game)

SUPER BOWL (PAGES 28-31) Rod Mar for Sports Illustrated (Seahawks); John Moore/Getty Images (stadium); Eric Lars Bakke for Sports Illustrated (Broncos); Donald Miralle for Sports Illustrated (Broncos tunnel)

MONSTER TRUCK (PAGES 32-37) David E. Klutho/Sports Illustrated

TRAVIS RICE (PAGES 38-39) Garrett W. Ellwood for Sports Illustrated

HEINZ FIELD (PAGES 40-43) Fred Vuich for Sports Illustrated (Steelers); David E. Klutho/Sports Illustrated (Penguins)

MLB STADIUMS (PAGES 44-45) Mark Cunningham/MLB Photos/Getty Images (Ferris Wheel); Marc Serota/Getty Images (bobbleheads); Doug Pensinger/Getty Images (rays); Abelimages/Getty Images (hotel)

HOCKEY GEAR (PAGES 46–49) Andy Marlin/NHLI/Getty Images (Brodeur action); Michael J. LeBrecht II for Spotrts Illustrated (Brodeur portraits); David E. Klutho/Sports Illustrated (hockey goal)

HALL OF FAME ARTIFACTS (PAGES 50-51) National Baseball Hall of Fame

SHOES (PAGES 52-55) Don Penny for Sports Illustrated (Adidas Adipure, Adidas Nitrocharge); Nathanial S. Butler/NBAE/Getty Images (Lopez); Garrett W. Elwood/NBAE/Getty Images (Robinson); Brad Mills/USA Today Sports (Forbath); Art Rickerby/Getty Images (Péle); Courtesy Nike (Bruin, Air Jordan); Puma (Puma King); Adidas (Predator, Adizero)

STANLEY CUP (PAGES 56-57) David Dow/NHLI/Getty Images (Stanley Cup); Dave Sandford/NHLI/Getty Images (Recchi); Walter Iooss Jr. for Sports Illustrated (Richard); Courtesy of sportscardforum.com (Cup closeup); David E. Klutho for Sports Illustrated (Messier); Courtesy Hockey Hall of Fame (St. Jacques); Susan Walsh/AP (Red Wings)

FOOTBALL (PAGES 58-61) David E. Klutho/Sports Illustrated (Making of Football); Lou Capozzola for Sports Illustrated (Crosby); Annmarie Avila/Sports Illustrated (Football)

CREDITS (PAGE 62) Heinz Kluetmeier for Sports Illustrated (Cabrera); Heinz Kluetmeier/Sports Illustrated (James); Robert Beck/Sports Illustrated (Wilson); Mark J. Terrill/AP (Puig)

BACK INSIDE COVER Andrew D. Bernstein/NBAE/Getty Images

BACK COVER David E. Klutho/Sports Illustrated (monster truck); Michael J. LeBrecht II for Sports Illustrated (Johnson); Zach Wolfe for Sports Illustrated (Johnson sneakers)

Winning Friends
NBA players Stephen Curry, Chris Paul, Kevin Durant, and James Harden (from left) catch up in the locker room before the 2014 All-Star game at Smoothie King Center in New Orleans, Louisiana.